T0159897

Greg McLeod is a BAFTA-award-winning illustrator and animator. He has worked with many lovely people and organizations, and his illustration work encompasses experimental personal projects through to product design, books and drawing on lollipop sticks to name a few. He won an award for the lollipop stick thing. Greg's children have had multiple pet rabbits, including Twitch, who was the living embodiment of the rabbit from *Monty Python and the Holy Grail*.

Liz Marvin is an editor and writer. She has also written *How to Be More Tree*, published by Michael O'Mara Books. She doesn't have any pets, but has named the pigeons that live outside her bedroom window.

THE
SECRET
LIVES
OF
ANIMALS

ILLUSTRATED BY GREG McLEOD

WRITTEN BY LIZ MARVIN

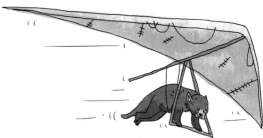

First published in Great Britain in 2020 by LOM Art, an imprint of
Michael O'Mara Books Limited
9 Lion Yard
Tremadoc Road
London SW4 7NQ

A CIP catalogue record for this book is available
from the British Library.

Papers used by Michael O'Mara Books Limited are natural,
recyclable products made from wood grown in sustainable
forests. The manufacturing processes conform to the
environmental regulations of the country of origin.

ISBN: 978-1-912785-23-0 in hardback print format
ISBN: 978-1-912785-24-7 in ebook format

1 2 3 4 5 6 7 8 9 10

Designed and typeset by Ana Bjezancevic and Barbara Ward

Printed in China

www.mombooks.com

INTRODUCTION

Our friends in the animal kingdom get up to some pretty surprising things. But while most of us know that foxes are cunning and dolphins are intelligent, have you ever stopped to think about the hidden talents of a wombat? Or that armadillos have a few more strings to their bow than simply doing a very good impression of an inflated bicycle helmet?

Do you know how toucans charm their mates? Or what sloths are actually really good at? Or what a horse might be able to tell about you? From the Amazon rainforest to the polar ice caps, from the Australian bush to the seabed, there's a lot more going on out there in the natural world than most of us realize.

Whether it's defending their home from unwelcome guests, tricking a competitor who might have an eye on their dinner or finding a way to avoid being dinner themselves, the furry, feathery and scaly inhabitants of our planet have learned to do all sorts of neat tricks and impressive acrobatics. From penguins to pythons, owls to octopuses and geckos to goats, read on to learn about some amazing animal skills that cast our fascinating wildlife in a whole new light. It turns out that a lot of animals are cleverer and far sneakier than we've given them credit for ...

5

RACCOONS

IF THERE WAS EVER AN ANIMAL THAT CAME DRESSED FOR THE PART, IT'S A RACCOON. THESE MASKED BANDITS HAVE BEEN SHOWN TO BE EXCELLENT LOCK PICKERS, AND CAPABLE OF REMEMBERING SOLUTIONS TO COMPLICATED PUZZLES. AND WHEN THEY EVENTUALLY GET SENT DOWN FOR THEIR CRIMES, THEIR STRIPY TAILS WILL MAKE THE PERFECT PRISON UNIFORM.

GIRAFFES

A LONG NECK: GREAT FOR EATING DINNER WHEN IT'S SERVED HIGH UP; APPRECIATING THE VIEW; FIGHTING (REALLY!). NOT SO GREAT FOR: DRINKING. THERE'S ONLY ONE WAY AROUND IT — SPREAD YOUR LEGS AND STICK YOUR BUM IN THE AIR. SO AWKWARD THAT A GIRAFFE ONLY STOPS TO DRINK EVERY FEW DAYS ... PROBABLY WHEN NO ONE ELSE IS WATCHING.

TOUCANS

AS PART OF THEIR MATING RITUAL, TOUCANS OFTEN GIVE EACH OTHER PRESENTS AND THROW FRUIT BACK AND FORTH BETWEEN THEIR BEAKS. SO, IF YOU'RE A GIRL TOUCAN AND YOU GET SMACKED IN THE FACE WITH A WET BIT OF GUAVA, GAME ON, APPARENTLY.

GIANT PANDAS

SOME MAY CALL THEM LAZY, BUT PANDAS SEE
IT MORE AS ... BAMBOO AND CHILL. THEIR
FAVOURITE FOOD IS LOW IN CALORIES, SO THEY
TAKE THINGS SLOW TO CONSERVE ENERGY. WITH
THE EXCEPTION OF SCENT MARKING, WHICH
THEY TAKE VERY SERIOUSLY BY PERFORMING
AN OUT-OF-CHARACTER ACROBATIC HANDSTAND
TO WEE AS HIGH UP A TREE AS POSSIBLE.

MEERKATS

THESE RIGHT-ON COOL CATS FORM THE ULTIMATE
WORKERS' COOPERATIVE. THEY LIVE UNDERGROUND
IN A NETWORK OF TUNNELS, SHARE PUPCARE AND
TAKE TURNS ACTING AS LOOKOUT. THEY HUNT
TOGETHER TOO, IN GANGS. AS THEY ARE UNDER
A FOOT TALL WITH A CUTE AND FLUFFY FACADE,
A MEERKAT GANG MIGHT NOT LOOK TOO SCARY,
BUT TOGETHER THEY ARE CAPABLE OF BRINGING
DOWN A SNAKE IF IT MESSES WITH THE CREW ...

PUFFINS

THESE LITTLE MEMBERS OF THE AUK FAMILY
SPEND MOST OF THEIR LIVES AT SEA, SO WHEN
THEY COME ASHORE TO BREED THEY ARE

READY FOR SOME CREATURE COMFORTS. THEY
PICK A COSY BURROW OVER A NEST, AND EVEN
SET ASIDE SPACE FOR A SEPARATE TOILET.

SEA OTTERS

THESE CUTE LITTLE WATER WEASELS ARE
STRONG SWIMMERS, CLEVER FORAGERS AND ...
ACCOMPLISHED JUGGLERS! THEY CAN MANAGE TWO
OR THREE PEBBLES AT A TIME, EVEN WITH THEIR
EYES CLOSED. AND THE STONE LOVE DOESN'T END
THERE — SOME HAVE BEEN KNOWN TO CARRY
AROUND THE SAME ONE THEIR WHOLE LIVES.

BORDER COLLIES

ON TOP OF THEIR IMPRESSIVE SHEEP-HERDING
SKILLS, THESE SUPER-SMART CANINES CAN
UNDERSTAND HUNDREDS OF DIFFERENT COMMANDS,
PERFORM COMPLICATED TASKS AND EVEN TAKE
PART IN GUINNESS WORLD RECORD ATTEMPTS.
WHEN STRIKER'S OWNER CHALLENGED HIM TO
WIND DOWN A CAR WINDOW AS FAST AS POSSIBLE,
HE DID IT IN 11.34 SECONDS ... BEFORE DRIVING
TO THE SHOP TO PICK UP MORE KIBBLE.

KINKAJOUS

THESE DOUBLE-JOINTED ACROBATS SUFFER FROM A
KEEN SWEET TOOTH AND A BIT OF AN IDENTITY
CRISIS. THEY'RE SOMETIMES CALLED HONEY
BEARS BECAUSE THEY RAID BEES' NESTS, WHILE
THEIR MONKEY-LIKE FACES MEAN THEY'RE OFTEN
MISTAKEN FOR PRIMATES. ACTUALLY, THEY'RE A
SORT OF RACCOON, WITH AN AMAZING TAIL THAT
LETS THEM PERFORM ALL SORTS OF AERIAL FEATS.

GECKOS.

GECKOS HAVE A PRETTY NEAT, IF SLIGHTLY
WEIRD, PARTY TRICK. SOME SPECIES SHED THEIR
TAILS IF CAUGHT BY A PREDATOR AND THE
DISEMBODIED TAIL CAN CARRY ON MOVING FOR
THIRTY MINUTES AFTER IT HAS LEFT ITS GECKO,
EVEN JUMPING THREE CENTIMETRES IN THE AIR.

RED PANDAS

THEIR ADORABLE FACES BELIE A DANGEROUS
MIND. THESE TALENTED CLIMBERS AND SWIMMERS
ARE ALSO SKILLED ESCAPE ARTISTS. THEY'VE
BEEN KNOWN TO CASUALLY BREAK OUT OF
ZOOS ALL OVER THE WORLD, WITH NO SECRET
TUNNELS OR MOTORBIKE STUNTS NEEDED.

ARMADILLOS

THEY MIGHT LOOK LIKE A CROSS BETWEEN A RAT
AND A BICYCLE HELMET, BUT ARMADILLOS HAVE
AN UNEXPECTED TRICK UP THEIR ARMOURED
SLEEVE. THEY COME WITH THEIR VERY OWN
LIFE JACKETS. IF AN ARMADILLO NEEDS TO GO
FOR A SWIM, IT CAN INFLATE ITS STOMACH TO
TWICE ITS USUAL SIZE FOR PERFECT BUOYANCY.

PARROTS

THESE AMAZING MIMICS CAN BE UTTER
ATTENTION SEEKERS. SNOWBALL THE DANCING
COCKATOO BECAME AN INTERNET SENSATION
AFTER HE SEEMED TO CHOREOGRAPH
HIS OWN DANCE ROUTINE — A DAZZLING
FOURTEEN-MOVE REPERTOIRE!

WOMBATS

THEY MIGHT LOOK LIKE SMALL, HAIRY BARRELS, BUT OBSTINATE WOMBATS ARE NOT TO BE MESSED WITH. IF ATTACKED BY A DINGO, THEY'LL BLOCK THEIR BURROW ENTRANCES WITH THEIR BODIES, BUM OUT. THEIR REAR ENDS ARE COVERED IN THICK, TOUGH SKIN AND THEIR TINY TAILS ARE HARD TO GRAB ONTO.

SEA LIONS

ALL SIX SPECIES OF SEA LIONS HAVE AN
AMAZING SENSE OF SMELL, HEARING AND
IMPRESSIVE UNDERWATER EYESIGHT.

RONAN THE CALIFORNIAN SEA LION ALSO HAS AN
EXCELLENT SENSE OF RHYTHM. SHE HAS BEEN
OBSERVED BOBBING HER HEAD IN TIME TO
MUSIC, MUCH LIKE A DAD AT A WEDDING DISCO.

HUMPBACK WHALES

THESE WHALES ARE INCORRIGIBLE SHOW-OFFS. THE MALES SING COMPLEX SONGS LASTING UP TO THIRTY MINUTES TO ATTRACT A MATE, WHICH SOUNDS LIKE THE WORST OPEN MIC NIGHT EVER. BUT AS THERE ARE BABY HUMPBACK WHALES, WE CAN ONLY ASSUME IT'S NOT AS OFF-PUTTING AS IT SOUNDS.

CAPYBARAS

IMAGINE A VERY BIG, SEMI-AQUATIC GUINEA
PIG AND YOU'LL BE PART OF THE WAY THERE
TO A CAPYBARA. THEY HAVE A PRACTICAL,
NO-NONSENSE ATTITUDE — PRETTY ESSENTIAL
WHEN YOU'RE ON THE MENU FOR MOST OF
SOUTH AMERICA'S LARGE PREDATORS. THEY
EVEN START THE DAY WITH A NUTRITIONAL
PORTION OF POO. THEIR OWN POO.

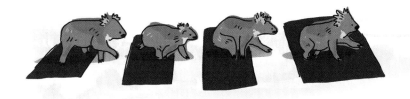

KOALAS

DON'T UNDERESTIMATE A KOALA, THEY ARE
SMARTER THAN YOU THINK. SURE, THEY ARE
ASLEEP MOST OF THE TIME, AND THEY MOVE
V-E-R-Y S-L-0-W-L-Y, BUT WHEN KOALA CROSSINGS
WERE BUILT IN BRISBANE TO IMPROVE THEIR
ROAD SAFETY, IT ONLY TOOK A FEW DAYS FOR
THEM TO GET THE HANG OF CROSSING LIKE PROS.

CHAMELEONS

WHEN A CHAMELEON WALKS, IT ROCKS
BACKWARDS AND FORWARDS, AS IF GETTING
READY TO START A RACE. THIS ODD WOBBLE
MIGHT BE ITS IMPRESSION OF A LEAF SWAYING
IN THE BREEZE IN AN EFFORT TO BLEND IN.
OR MAYBE CHAMELEONS ARE JUST DANCING
TO A RHYTHM ONLY THEY CAN HEAR.

TIGERS

THE LION ROARS, THE WOLF HOWLS, THE TIGER SAYS ... 'POOK'. WHILE THEY MIGHT BE BETTER KNOWN AS JUNGLE HUNTERS, OR FOR BEING THE FACE OF SUGARY BREAKFAST CEREALS,

TIGERS ARE ALSO GREAT MIMICS. AND THEY USE
THIS SKILL TO DEVIOUS ADVANTAGE, IMITATING
THE NOISE OF A SAMBAR DEER TO DRAW
IT OUT INTO THE OPEN AND AMBUSH IT.

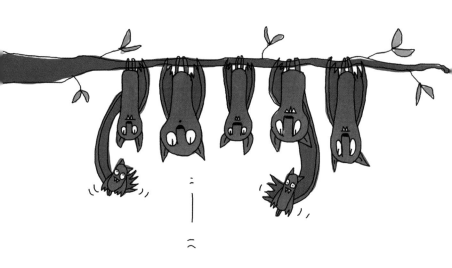

BATS

BATS ARE DEXTEROUS FLYERS BUT YOU WOULDN'T CALL THEM GROUNDED ... THEIR LEG BONES ARE SO DELICATE THAT THEY CAN'T ACTUALLY WALK, SO THEY TAKE OFF BY SUDDENLY DROPPING FROM THEIR PERCHES. THEY EVEN GIVE BIRTH UPSIDE DOWN. LUCKILY THEY'RE PRETTY GOOD AT CATCHING.

OCTOPUSES

THESE BRAINIACS ARE IMPRESSIVE PROBLEM
SOLVERS AND MULTITASKERS. EACH OF THEIR
ARMS (DON'T CALL THEM TENTACLES!) CAN
FUNCTION INDEPENDENTLY. IMAGINE BEING
ABLE TO TYPE, KNIT, READ A BOOK AND
LOOK FOR YOUR HOUSEKEYS IN THE BOTTOM
OF YOUR BAG ALL AT THE SAME TIME.

KOMODO DRAGONS

THESE TERRIFYING HUNTERS MAKE CROCODILES LOOK AMATEUR. THEY WAIT PATIENTLY FOR PRETTY MUCH ANY PASSING MAMMAL, ATTACK IT WITH THEIR POWERFUL, VENOMOUS JAWS AND, IF THEIR VICTIM GETS AWAY, THEN THEY CAN TRACK IT FOR MILES USING THEIR TONGUE TO 'TASTE' THE AIR. CREEPY.

BALL PYTHONS

THIS SHY, NON-VENOMOUS SNAKE CAN CURL UP
INTO A BALL WITH JUST ITS NOSE POKING OUT.
WHEN IT'S ALL COILED UP, THIS PYTHON CAN
BE ROLLED AROUND LIKE A BASKETBALL (LIKE
A BASKETBALL WITH LIGHTNING REFLEXES AND
THIRTY-FIVE VERY POINTY TEETH, THAT IS).

GORILLAS

THEY MIGHT LOOK LIKE THE RUGBY FORWARDS OF THE ANIMAL KINGDOM, BUT DON'T BE FOOLED BY THEIR MASSIVE HAIRY BULK — THESE GUYS ARE SERIOUSLY INTELLIGENT.

THEY KNOW HOW TO USE A STICK TO MEASURE
WATER DEPTH AND COLLECT FOOD, AND EVEN
MAKE LITTLE BAMBOO LADDERS FOR THEIR BABIES.

Squirrels

THESE FLUFFY-TAILED RODENTS MAY LOOK THE
PICTURE OF FLEET-FOOTED INDUSTRY, BUT
SOMETIMES THIS IS JUST AN ELABORATE PLOY
TO ENSURE NO ONE GETS NEAR THEIR NUTS.
IF THEY THINK THEY'RE BEING WATCHED,
THEY'LL PRETEND TO BURY A NUT, BUT REALLY
SPIRIT IT AWAY TO A NEW, SECRET LOCATION.

TRIGGERFISH

THEY MIGHT LOOK LIKE THEY ARE WEARING AN
AWFUL LOT OF MAKEUP, BUT TRIGGERFISH ARE
MORE THAN JUST A PRETTY FACE. RELATIVELY
SPEAKING (THEY ARE STILL FISH), THEY'RE PRETTY
SMART — THEY HAVE LEARNED TO BLAST WATER
AT SPIKY SEA URCHINS TO FLIP THEM OVER AND
GET AT THEIR SOFT AND VULNERABLE UNDERSIDE.

MANTA RAYS

THESE UNDERWATER FLYING BLANKETS ARE
IMPRESSIVE AQUATIC ACROBATS AND MUCH SMARTER
THAN THEY LOOK. ONE FAMOUS RAY, FRECKLES,
ONCE FLAGGED DOWN SOME FRIENDLY DIVERS AND
WAITED PATIENTLY WHILE THEY REMOVED SOME
FISH HOOKS THAT HAD GOT STUCK IN HER SKIN.

CHIMPS

THESE GREAT APES ARE PRETTY DARN
CLEVER AND THEY WANT YOU TO KNOW
ABOUT IT. CONGO THE CHIMP LEARNED TO
DRAW AND PAINT, AND BECAME FAMOUS
FOR HIS 'LYRICAL ABSTRACT IMPRESSIONISM'
— PICASSO WAS REPORTEDLY A FAN.

PLATYPUSES

A BEAK LIKE A DUCK'S; FUR LIKE AN OTTER;
BIG OLD WEBBED FEET; A FLAT TAIL; POINTY
ANKLE SPIKES THAT DELIVER POISON AND NO
TEETH, SO THEY USE STONES TO GRIND THEIR
FOOD INSTEAD. IS THIS STRANGE CREATURE ...
   FRANKENBEAVER?! NOPE, IT'S A PLATYPUS.

RATS

IT STANDS TO REASON THAT A GROUP OF RATS
IS OFTEN CALLED A MISCHIEF. SOCIAL, AND WITH
AMAZING MEMORIES, THEY ALSO LOVE TO PLAY
HIDE-AND-SEEK. THEY SWITCH BETWEEN BEING
THE HIDER AND THE SEEKER — AND EMIT
A JOYFUL, RATTY SQUEAL WHEN THEY WIN.

ELEPHANTS

FAMOUS FOR NEVER FORGETTING, AND FOR
HAVING MASSIVE EARS. SO IT'S NOT A SURPRISE
THAT THEY HAVE GREAT HEARING. SLIGHTLY
MORE SURPRISING IS THAT AN ELEPHANT CAN
ALSO HEAR THROUGH ITS FEET — DETECTING
VIBRATIONS THAT THEN TRAVEL UP THROUGH
ITS BODY AND INTO ITS MIDDLE EAR.

CROCODILES

JUST WHEN YOU THOUGHT THESE DEVIOUS
DINOSAURS COULDN'T GET ANY MORE UNNERVING,
THEY'VE NOW BEEN OBSERVED LURING
UNSUSPECTING BIRDS BY BALANCING A NEST
OF TWIGS ON THEIR SNOUTS AND REMAINING
STILL FOR HOURS, READY TO POUNCE.

GENTOO PENGUINS

THESE GUYS MAKE THE CUTEST COUPLES IN THE ANTARCTIC. THE MALE WOOS HIS MATE BY PRESENTING HER WITH THE SHINIEST PEBBLE HE CAN FIND. HE ALSO MAKES A TRUMPETING NOISE, WHICH IS APPARENTLY VERY ATTRACTIVE IF YOU'RE A FEMALE PENGUIN.

KANGAROOS

MALE KANGAROOS HAVE SERIOUSLY IMPRESSIVE
MUSCLE TONE, CAN COVER UP TO TWENTY-FIVE
FEET IN A SINGLE LEAP, BOX EACH OTHER TO
ESTABLISH WHO THE TOUGHEST 'ROO IS AND
HAVE BEEN OBSERVED FLEXING THEIR ARMS TO
ATTRACT FEMALES. IT'S NOT KNOWN WHETHER
FEMALE KANGAROOS CAN ROLL THEIR EYES.

PINK RIVER DOLPHINS

THIS FRESHWATER DOLPHIN FROM THE AMAZON IS, LET'S BE HONEST, NOT THE MOST ATTRACTIVE AQUATIC MAMMAL. BUT IT'S NOT BOTHERED. POSSIBLY BECAUSE IT'S TOO BUSY GETTING HIGH. YES, THAT'S RIGHT. THEY SEEM TO DELIBERATELY SEEK OUT PUFFERFISH FOR THEIR POWERFUL HALLUCINOGENIC TOXINS.

WOLVES

IF ANY ANIMAL NEEDS NEW PR REPRESENTATION,
IT'S WOLVES. THEY MIGHT BE FAMOUS FOR
THEIR CHILLING HOWLS, BUT THEY ARE MORE
SENSITIVE THAN THEY GET CREDIT FOR.
THEY ARE IN FACT SKILLED COMMUNICATORS,
AND HAVE AN IMPRESSIVE RANGE OF FACIAL
EXPRESSIONS. IT'S NOT ALL ABOUT HUFFING
AND PUFFING AND BLOWING THINGS DOWN.

FLAMINGOES

THESE MAGNIFICENTLY ATTIRED BIRDS POSE
REGALLY AROUND THE EDGES OF SHALLOW
LAKES. UNTIL DINNER TIME, THAT IS, WHEN
THEY DUNK THEIR HEADS UPSIDE DOWN
IN THE WATER, SWEEPING THEM FROM
SIDE TO SIDE AND VIGOROUSLY SNORTING
WATER THROUGH THEIR BEAKS TO FILTER
OUT THEIR MEAL. EXTRAORDINARY.

CAMELS

IT'S THE HUMPS THAT GET THE PRESS, BUT
CAMELS HAVE VERY IMPRESSIVE NOSTRILS, WHICH
THEY USE TO RETAIN WATER VAPOUR AND
CAN CLOSE IF IT GETS TOO DUSTY OUT IN THE
DESERT. THESE GENIAL UNGULATES LIKE TO HANG
AROUND IN GROUPS OF ABOUT THIRTY AND SAY
HI BY BLOWING IN EACH OTHER'S FACES.

BEAVERS

THE DIY ENTHUSIASTS OF THE ANIMAL KINGDOM, THESE INDUSTRIOUS LITTLE GUYS CAN CHANGE THEIR ENVIRONMENT LIKE NO OTHER ANIMAL — APART FROM HUMANS. BEAVERS BUILD THEIR LODGES WITH A SECRET LITTLE UNDERWATER BACK DOOR, FOR CONVENIENT ACCESS AND TO DETER PREDATORS WHO DON'T LIKE GETTING WET.

FOXES

IT SEEMS THAT FOXES ARE EVEN MORE CUNNING THAN WE MAY HAVE THOUGHT. THEY HAVE A SORT OF INBUILT 'COMPASS', WHICH MEANS THEY CAN SEE A RING OF SHADOW ON THEIR RETINAS THAT DARKENS NEAR MAGNETIC NORTH AND HELPS THEM JUDGE THE DISTANCE TO THEIR PREY. GOOD NEWS FOR FOXES; BAD NEWS FOR BUNNIES.

TAPIRS

POOR TAPIRS GET SERIOUS SIDE-EYE FROM THE REST OF THE ANIMAL KINGDOM. THEY ARE MOST CLOSELY RELATED TO HORSES AND RHINOS BUT LOOK MORE LIKE PIGS, AND HAVE A STUBBY TRUNK-LIKE NOSE. HOWEVER, IN NATURE, IT'S ALL ABOUT WHAT YOU CAN DO AND THE TAPIR CAN HIDE IN WATER WHEN THREATENED, USING ITS WEIRD NOSE AS A SNORKEL.

HUMMINGBIRDS

HUMMINGBIRDS ARE THE ONLY BIRDS THAT
CAN FLY BACKWARDS, THEY'RE HARD WORKERS
AND THEY HAVE EXCELLENT MEMORIES. THEY
AREN'T, HOWEVER, PARTICULARLY NEIGHBOURLY.
THEY WILL HAPPILY STEAL BUILDING MATERIAL
FROM NEARBY NESTS AND RARELY SIGN
FOR EACH OTHER'S AMAZON DELIVERIES.

LIONS

LIONS HAVE A HIDDEN SCENT GLAND BETWEEN
THEIR TOES, WHICH IS ONE OF THE LESS
INTIMIDATING REASONS WHY THEY LIKE TO
SCRATCH TREES — AS WELL AS SHARPENING
AND CLEANING THEIR CLAWS, THEY ARE
ALSO MARKING THEIR TERRITORY.

BURROWING OWLS

THESE OWLS ESCHEW NESTS IN TREES AND
BUILDINGS FOR A MORE OFF-GRID, SUSTAINABLE
LIFESTYLE. THEY DIG BURROWS (OR RECYCLE
ONES MADE BY OTHER ANIMALS) AND, BEFORE
LAYING EGGS, GENEROUSLY SCATTER THEIR
OWN POO AROUND THE ENTRANCE TO ENSURE
A HOME-GROWN SUPPLY OF DUNG BEETLES
AND OTHER INSECTS IN THEIR GARDEN.

WOLVERINES

FAMOUS FOR THEIR SHARP CLAWS AND HUNTING
SKILLS, AND THE BEST-KNOWN OF ALL THE
X-MEN, THESE FEARSOME LITTLE BEASTS CAN
BRING DOWN PREY LARGER THAN THEY ARE
BY HIDING BEHIND ROCKS, READY TO POUNCE.
DESPITE THEIR COOL NAME, HOWEVER, WOLVERINES
ARE NOT WOLVES OR EVEN BEARS — THEY ARE
BASICALLY LARGE WEASELS. SOMEHOW THEY
DON'T SEEM QUITE SO INTIMIDATING NOW.

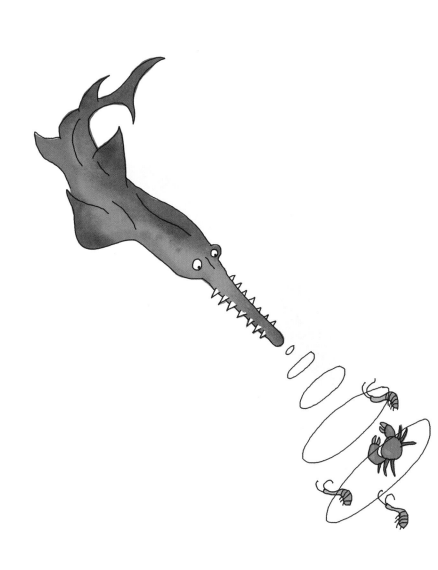

SAWFISH

IT MIGHT NOT SEEM LIKE THERE'S MUCH
THAT'S SUBTLE ABOUT A FISH WITH A LARGE
BREADKNIFE STUCK TO ITS NOSE, BUT ACTUALLY
THESE RAYS ARE MORE SENSITIVE THAN YOU
THINK. AS WELL AS BEING USEFUL FOR WARDING
OFF SHARK ATTACKS AND SLICING A BAGUETTE,
THEIR SNOUTS HAVE ELECTRORECEPTORS USED
TO DETECT THE FAINT HEARTBEATS OF THEIR
FAVOURITE CRAB AND SHRIMP SNACKS.

POLAR BEARS

EVERYONE NEEDS A DAY OFF SOMETIMES, IT SEEMS, EVEN RELENTLESS PREDATORS. OCCASIONALLY, THESE ARCTIC BAD BOYS SWAP SEAL-HUNTING FOR A SPOT OF LUGE — THEY'VE BEEN OBSERVED GETTING TOGETHER TO SLIDE AROUND ON AN ICY SLOPE, AND ENJOYING A LIGHT-HEARTED WRESTLING MATCH.

101

NARWHALS

THE MALE OF THE SPECIES SPORTS A LONG TUSK
(ACTUALLY A TOOTH!), WHICH LOOKS INCONVENIENT
AT BEST, AND DANGEROUSLY POINTY. HOWEVER,
THIS PROTUBERANCE IS NOT A WEAPON — IT'S
POROUS AND FULL OF NERVES, WHICH ALLOWS
THE NARWHAL TO PICK UP USEFUL SEA INFO, LIKE
WATER PRESSURE, TEMPERATURE AND MOTION.

BASSIAN THRUSHES

THIS UNASSUMING LITTLE BIRD FROM EASTERN AUSTRALIA IS NOT ABOVE USING ANY TACTIC TO GET ITS EARTHWORM PREY ... INCLUDING FARTING ON THEM. IT RELEASES GAS ONTO LEAF LITTER, WHICH APPARENTLY SHOCKS AND DISGUSTS THE WORMS SO MUCH THEY MOVE, REVEALING WHERE THEY ARE.

SUN BEARS

SUN BEARS HAVE A BIT OF A BRANDING ISSUE.
CONTRARY TO THEIR NAME, THEY ACTUALLY
ONLY COME OUT AT NIGHT (IN FACT THEIR
NAME REFERS TO THE SNAZZY GOLD PATCH OF
FUR UNDER THEIR CHINS). SLEEPING DURING
THE DAY IS NOT AN EASY BUSINESS, AND
THEY CLEVERLY BUILD LITTLE BEAR-SIZED
NESTS UP IN THE TREES OUT OF BRANCHES.

BEARDED DRAGONS

THESE TINY DINOSAURS GET THEIR NAME FROM THEIR ABILITY TO PUFF UP THE SPIKY SKIN UNDER THEIR THROATS, WHICH THEY DO TO TRY TO LOOK A BIT SCARY. THEY ARE ALSO KNOWN TO WAVE SLOWLY WHEN THEY BUMP INTO ANOTHER DRAGON THEY RECOGNIZE, WHICH COULD BE FRIENDLY, BUT ACTUALLY LOOKS A LITTLE BIT CONDESCENDING.

ORCAS

BEING AN AQUATIC MAMMAL CAN BE CHALLENGING. BREATHING MAY BE BASIC FOR US, BUT NOT FOR ORCAS. THEY ACTUALLY HAVE TO DECIDE WHEN TO DO IT. IF THEY NOD OFF AND FORGET THEN THEY'LL DROWN. SO ONLY ONE SIDE OF THEIR BRAIN GOES TO SLEEP AT A TIME!

GREEN-and-BLACK POISON DART FROGS

THIS TROPICAL FROG PIGGYBACKS ITS TADPOLES AND
POPS THEM IN A WATER-FILLED HOLE UP A TREE,
CREATING A COMPLEX MENTAL MAP THAT ALLOWS
IT TO REMEMBER THE CORRECT TREE AMONG MANY
THOUSANDS IN THE FOREST. SOMETHING TO THINK
ABOUT NEXT TIME YOU CAN'T FIND YOUR KEYS.

MYANMAR SNUB-NOSED MONKEYS

THIS VERY RARE SPECIES OF MONKEY SPENDS RAINY DAYS MOSTLY SITTING WITH ITS HEAD BETWEEN ITS LEGS. BUT DON'T WORRY, IT'S NOT SAD. IT'S JUST THAT, WHEN EXPOSED, ITS UPTURNED NOSE LETS IN THE WATER AND MAKES THE MONKEY SNEEZE. BLESS YOU.

GOATS

THIS JUMPER-MUNCHING LOT ARE AS CLEVER
AS DOGS AND JUST AS SOCIAL, TOO. THEY CAN
BUILD RELATIONSHIPS WITH THEIR HUMAN
BUDDIES AND LEARN TO COME WHEN CALLED.
THEY'RE ALSO VERY IN TUNE WITH EACH OTHER
— EVEN COPYING THEIR HERD-MATES' ACCENTS.

ACORN WOODPECKERS

THESE HOARDERS ARE COMPLETELY OBSESSED WITH NUTS. THEY BORE HOLES IN TREES, FENCE POSTS, TELEGRAPH POLES AND HOUSES INTO WHICH THEY POKE THEIR ACORNS. A TEAM OF WOODPECKERS CAN STORE THOUSANDS OF NUTS IN WHAT'S KNOWN AS A GRANARY TREE, WHICH THEY EAT THROUGH THE WINTER — PROVIDED THOSE PESKY SQUIRRELS DON'T FIND OUT ...

SLOTHS

EVERYONE GOES ON ABOUT HOW LAZY SLOTHS
ARE, HOW SLOWLY THEY MOVE — AND THE
SLOTHS HAVE HAD ENOUGH. YES, THEY MIGHT
SLEEP FOR AT LEAST TEN HOURS A DAY AND
IT TAKES THEM AGES TO CLIMB A TREE, BUT
THEY'D LIKE YOU TO KNOW THEY ARE GREAT
SWIMMERS. FRONT CRAWL, SINCE YOU ASKED.

CROWS

CROWS ARE CLEVER, SOCIABLE AND DEXTEROUS
— THEY'VE EVEN BEEN SPOTTED USING TOOLS.
BUT NEVER CROSS A CROW — NOT ONLY ARE
THEY ASSOCIATED IN WESTERN CULTURES WITH
DEATH AND BAD OMENS, THEY CAN RECOGNIZE
HUMAN FACES AND THEY WON'T FORGET
WHAT YOU DID WITH THAT BIRDFEEDER ...

HORSES

HORSES CAN SLEEP STANDING UP IF THEY
WANT, LOCKING THEIR LEGS SO THEY DON'T
FALL OVER. THEY ARE PRETTY GOOD AT
READING PEOPLE AND RECOGNIZING OUR FACIAL
EXPRESSIONS, TOO; THEY CAN EVEN REMEMBER
A PERSON'S EMOTIONAL STATE AND ADAPT
THEIR BEHAVIOUR ACCORDINGLY. ESSENTIALLY,
A HORSE MAY WELL BE HUMOURING YOU.

INDEX

Giant pandas
p.12

Giraffes
p.8

Goats
p.117

Gorillas
p.54

Green-and-black
poison dart frogs p.112

Horses
p.125

Hummingbirds
p.91

Humpback whales
p.37

Kangaroos
p.74

Kinkajous
p.23

Koalas
p.41

Komodo dragons
p.51

Lions
p.92

Manta rays
p.61

Meerkats
p.15

Myanmar snub-
nosed monkeys p.115

Narwhals
p.103

Octopuses
p.48

Orcas
p.111

Parrots
p.31